Contents

Page 1. Introduction

Page 2. Oxbridge
    Why Oxbridge?
    Oxford or Cambridge?
    Which College?

Page 8. How can I get into Oxbridge?
    Who is Oxbridge looking for?

Page 11. The Application Process
    What does Oxbridge want?
    Structuring your statement
    Final tips

Page 15. The BMAT
    What is it?
    How can I prepare?
    Final tips

Page 19. Interviews
    What are Interviewers looking for?
    How can I prepare?
    Final tips

Page 29. Resources & Websites

Introduction

The Universities of Oxford and Cambridge or 'Oxbridge' as they are collectively known have existed for over 800 years. Together they have educated a significant number of leading politicians, scientists, thinkers, writers and medical experts, with a reputation extending to every corner of the globe. This reputation has sometimes been labelled as 'elitist' and when combined with the competition and mystery surrounding Oxbridge admissions it's understandable why some consider even the thought of applying to Oxbridge daunting.

However, although there is no doubting that Oxbridge has a certain prestige, it is important to bear in mind that they are both 'just' universities. I wrote this guide to illustrate this and to show students who may or may not have considered Oxford or Cambridge that one of these universities could well be the place for them. Everybody who has experienced or been involved with the Oxbridge selection process will have their own view of what optimises your application. Here I present a synopsis of what I believe to be the key points and principles of the process based upon my discussions with Oxbridge academics, current medical students and my own personal experience.

I hope that 'Oxbridge Medicine: The Applicant's Guide' will show you that Oxbridge is indeed socially diverse and non-exclusive. It will give you an insight into the Universities, discussing their similarities, differences, strengths and weaknesses, whilst also exploring their collegiate systems. It will outline the application process itself, providing a step-by-step walkthrough that explains and advises you on your path to Oxbridge, in addition to describing all the resources you need to maximise your chances of entry.

The process is tough and competitive, but with the right preparation you can submit a credible application and stand an excellent chance of success – why not turn the page and get started?

Oxbridge

Oxford and Cambridge are the two oldest and most prestigious universities in Britain, sharing a global reputation for academic excellence, in teaching as well as research. In particular, the medical course at each establishment is outstanding. Here are some benefits of an Oxbridge medical education:

Critical Thinking: Oxbridge won't simply teach you medicine; it will teach you how to think. The course is designed to provide you with an understanding of medical science and scientific methodology, equipping you with the ability to critically assess scientific arguments, tackle problems and devise ideas of your own. Medicine is a rapidly changing field: rather than simply being trained to fit a niche that exists at the moment, you will learn to become someone capable of shaping the development of medicine in the future.

Teaching: The 'tutorial' or 'supervision' system as it is referred to in Oxford and Cambridge respectively makes for an entirely different learning experience. It comprises small-group or near one-on-one teaching sessions with tutors (or supervisors) outside of lectures. These tutors are frequently the global leaders in their respective fields, making your tutorials with them a unique and privileged experience that will deepen your understanding far beyond the standard curriculum, exposing you to the complexities and controversies that lie at the forefront of medical science.

Colleges: Oxford and Cambridge are comprised of a central University and a number of colleges where students live, eat and socialise. This collegiate system allows you to become part of a unique and tightly knit community. Because each college has a different personality, with particular strengths, interests or talents this means that you can expect to find a college that truly suits you. Furthermore each college has students studying a variety of disciplines, bringing you into contact with people you otherwise might never have got to know - engineers, historians, philosophers and others - whose disciplines will broaden your understanding of medicine.

Research: Research opportunities at Oxbridge are unrivalled, with both universities offering laboratory placements in the third year of study. Here you are given complete independence, being able to devise and perform your own experiments, and work side by side with some of the most influential biomedical scientists in the world.

Course structure: Medicine at Oxbridge is divided into a preclinical course (years one to three) and a clinical course (years four to six). This ensures that prior to engaging with patients you have a firm grounding in medical science and the workings of the body. Following the preclinical course you are given the opportunity to move to another university for clinical study, to carry out research and attain a PhD, or even to leave Oxbridge with a Bachelor of Arts undergraduate degree in the medical sciences, allowing you to pursue other career options should you wish. Such flexibility is unparalleled.

What are the drawbacks? Simple – Oxbridge is demanding and intense. It will push you beyond your comfort zone and challenge you both academically and personally. Whether this is actually a drawback though depends on you and what you want from university.

Student profile: Why did you apply to Oxbridge?

For me, applying to Cambridge was quite a reluctant decision. I wasn't sure whether the heavily scientific course would really suit me, I didn't know if I wanted to move that far away from home, and above all I was really unsure that I would fit in at Cambridge at all. In the end I decided to include it as one of my applications, having warmed to the city, the student representatives and the teaching staff on an open day, thinking – what's the worst that could happen?

One of my big worries was the lack of early patient contact at Oxbridge: for me, a major motivation for studying to be a Doctor was the chance to work so closely with real people. However, I've come to appreciate how effective it is to focus on the basic medical science, compounding that knowledge before you try to deal with patients.

Perhaps most significantly, however, I was just worried that I wouldn't fit in at Cambridge. No one in my family has studied at Oxbridge, and frankly I was concerned that everyone there would be either 'geeks' or 'posh'. I couldn't have been more wrong. Of course, there is a great mixture of all types of people around at Cambridge, but the vast majority are completely normal, down to earth people who want to have a great university experience, not just to study every hour of the day. So whether you are a high flying sportsman, a keen musician or a hard party-goer, you will be sure to find lots of like minded people in Cambridge.

When I arrived at university I was also convinced that I would be the bottom of the class, and really did not deserve to be at Cambridge at all. It was comforting, however, to find that nearly everyone around me felt the same way! You are offered so much support, both personally and academically, really helping you to achieve your full potential.

Dan, St. John's College, Cambridge

Oxford or Cambridge?

Although similar, Oxford and Cambridge do have subtle differences:

Initially, the structure of the course at both universities is comparable. The first and second year constitute the preclinical course in medical sciences, where you cover subjects including anatomy, biochemistry, physiology, pharmacology, pathology and neuroscience. Assessment of these subjects is by essay writing, practicals, short-answer questions and on-line examinations. As you will find later on in this guide, the emphasis on the communication and thinking skills provided by essay writing carries through to the admissions process where colleges may look favourably upon students studying an essay-based A-level or with evidence of strong writing skills.

In the third year both universities allow you to pick your subject of choice to explore further. At Oxford there are around five options available, most of which are associated with the medical sciences. In Cambridge there is more variety, with courses ranging from astrophysics to zoology, allowing you to pursue a broader selection of subjects should you wish to do so.

Following year three, years four to six constitute the clinical course where you are trained in patient investigation, management and care, rotating between hospitals whilst also performing lab work and attending lectures.

It is important to realise that if you are offered a place to study medicine at Oxford or Cambridge, this does not include the clinical part of the course. In the third year at both universities you must re-apply to different medical schools across the country (mostly in London) for a clinical place – you are guaranteed a place, but it may not necessarily be at Oxbridge. The reason for this is that the Oxbridge clinical schools are smaller than their preclinical equivalents, meaning that some students must study elsewhere. This is not necessarily a disadvantage as it provides you with an opportunity to study at two universities across the six years rather than just one, indeed most students who do leave do so out of choice. One important difference between the two universities is that at Oxford there are clinical places for most preclinical students, whereas at Cambridge there are only clinical places for around half of a preclinical year group. This means that at Cambridge it is less likely that you will be able to keep your place should you want to.

Moving beyond academia, both Oxford and Cambridge are unique and historic towns to live in. Both have a large number of students from diverse backgrounds, with a range of societies and events that cater for most tastes. Notably, Oxford is a significantly larger town, with more restaurants, shops and nightclubs, giving you more choice, people and possibilities. In contrast Cambridge is smaller but more homely, with almost everything being within a ten minute cycle of a centrally located college. Which university you prefer of course depends on your own interests and personality. It is advised that you visit Oxford and Cambridge on their open days, and talk to students and tutors to help you make your decision.

Student profile: Why did you choose Cambridge over Oxford?

I chose to apply to Cambridge for many reasons. Cambridge offered a greater number of places to read Medicine. Seeing as though it is such a competitive subject, I thought it made sense for me to apply to a place where the medical intake is higher. Having spoken to medical students already at Cambridge, I got the feeling that it was an academically challenging yet still very enjoyable place to study. Following that, I visited the university on the Open Day and what really appealed to me was the small-town and amicable feel of the place. Together with the fact that Cambridge is an exceptional academic institution, I instantly knew that this is where I wanted to apply.

Kartik, Gonville and Caius College, Cambridge

Student profile: Why did you choose Oxford over Cambridge?

I decided to apply to Oxford instead of Cambridge for several reasons. When I visited Oxford it came across as a more traditional and yet livelier town than Cambridge, and I thought I'd have a more enjoyable time there. From an academic standpoint the smaller year size in Oxford was also appealing as it meant we would be taught in smaller groups. Finally the Oxford clinical school was renowned for being the best in the UK.

Jennifer, St. Edmund Hall, Oxford

Which College?

The college you pick will influence where you live, the people you meet, how you're taught and even what you eat. It's therefore important that you spend time and choose carefully. One method is to first narrow down your options based on prospectuses and online resources, and then visit your final choices on the university open day.

To gain an initial overview of the different colleges, read the official university and student based prospectuses, the websites for which can be found in the 'Resources and Websites' section of this guide. Here you will want to be considering factors such as the size of the college – do you prefer a small, tightly knit community or a larger one with a more students to meet? Location is also important – would you prefer a college near the medical departments or the centre of town or one away from the busy town centre? Is accommodation provided for all three years of your undergraduate degree? Is it a single sex college? Does it have the necessary facilities for you to pursue your extracurricular interests? Importantly, does the college have an environment that will foster academic success - such as an active medical society and a large number of medical tutors? If it does the competition and the quality of students applying could be higher. Another factor that could influence your university life is the wealth of your college; Trinity College Cambridge for example is the richest Oxbridge college, providing its students with healthy book and travel grants, reduced accommodation costs, and strong overall financial support. Finally, what are the college's strengths and interests? Is it sporty or musical? And does this suit you?

Once you have narrowed down your choices you should try to visit the colleges – meet the tutors, talk to current students, see the grounds and gain a feel for the college's ambiance. This forms the primary basis for many applicants' decisions and should make a significant contribution to yours, after all it is your one chance to really sample the place you may be living and working in for the next three to six years.

Your choice of college will be a very personal decision and one based on many considerations. When deciding, you should appreciate that although colleges have different numbers of places for medicine, there are mechanisms in place to ensure that choosing any given one will not significantly alter your chance of being accepted. In fact, a significant proportion of candidates submit an 'open' application, whereby the university automatically allocates you a college for interview. If you are unsure about which college to apply to this is certainly an option. Furthermore as a result of the admissions process, even if you do select a college, your actual offer may well be from another one. It's therefore important to bear in mind that the vast majority of your medical education will be in the university departments with the entire year cohort rather than your college, and that every Oxbridge college has its strengths and attractions. Indeed, your success and experience of university will depend on what you do, wherever you go, rather than on where you gain a place.

Student profile: How did you pick your college?

I picked my college by first reading across the prospectus for colleges that I thought would suit my personality. I narrowed them down and then on the open day visited my shortlist of colleges. It became very clear on the day which college I wanted to apply to.

I ended up I choosing Hertford College because of its reputation for being friendly and progressive, and its work-hard play-hard attitude. I also liked the openness and encouragement that they showed to students from a state school background, like myself, this became particularly clear when I met the students and tutors at the college on their open day.

Rhodri, Hertford College, Oxford

Student profile: How did you pick your college?

I visited Cambridge during my Easter holidays of Lower Sixth and also went to a Cambridge Open Day. As soon as I walked into St John's, I instantly liked it; the buildings looked majestic and the grounds were stunning! On doing a bit more research, I found that the facilities St John's had for sport and music were extensive and there was a very diverse range of societies as well. As a medical student, I was also impressed by the very friendly and approachable medical staff. Moreover, I found the resources for medics were very generous with large book grants available and an extremely well-stocked library.

All in all, I chose St John's as it was a large, diverse community with extensive facilities and great resources for medicine.

Vishal, St. John's College, Cambridge

How can I get into Oxbridge?

A simple question that has no simple answer. Getting into Oxbridge is difficult, and involves a multi-step process:

Step 1: Decide where you want to go
Step 2: Improve your extra-curricular profile
Step 3: Fill in the application forms
Step 4: Take the BioMedical Admissions Test
Step 5: Be interviewed

If you approach each step strategically, and prepare for it appropriately, you can and will maximise your chances of getting in. This guide attempts to demystify the secrets surrounding Oxbridge admissions, and show you how to approach the application process.

Student profile: What activities did you get involved in at school and how did these assist with your application?

Given the nature of the secondary school that I attended, the part of the UCAS form that I worried about most was 'extra-curricular activities'. With no sports teams, and few, if any organised academic clubs on offer, I felt like it would be impossible to stand out in my Oxford application. However, the interviewers were very considerate and understanding of my position, and instead focused on the enthusiasm and passion for medicine that I was able to show through simple things such as my reading around the subject and developing an interest in current medical issues. Without the necessary connections I was unable to come by hospital work experience easily, but volunteering in both my neighbouring elderly care home and spending time with local funeral directors provided me with an equally invaluable insight into healthcare in action. As well as giving me experiences that reinforced my ambition to study medicine, these placements provided me with material that I could draw upon in my interview. My advice to you would be: don't get put off by a lack of help and encouragement from school – the medical school is looking for someone with a genuine enthusiasm for the subject, not UCAS points!

Charlie, Exeter College, Oxford

Who is Oxbridge looking for?

Oxbridge receives thousands of applications every year from motivated students with plenty of A*'s at GCSEs and A's at A levels. If you want to get in you'll obviously need to demonstrate intellectual potential to benefit from a place, but in addition to this Oxbridge want to know that you will bring more to university and college life than a strong performance in the exams at the end of the year.

This could be as simple as having a particular skill, interest or talent that you've developed over the past few years; an outstanding academic record, playing sport or a musical instrument to a very high level, or a passionate interest in medicine or research illustrated by a wide range of work experiences accompanied by reading.

If you feel like none of the above apply to you though – don't worry. There is always time to improve, and a weak extra-curricular profile can easily be compensated for by a strong performance in the later stages of the Oxbridge application, namely the BMAT and the interview. Below are some activities that might make you a more attractive Oxbridge candidate:

Reading: This is relatively easy to add to your extra-curricular base and demonstrates your interest in medicine, furthermore, in interviews you are sometimes questioned on recent developments in the medical field. Try to read magazines such as Scientific American, New Scientist or the Student BMJ, and books including the 'Selfish Gene' by Richard Dawkins.

Research: Any research you undertake at this stage will look impressive, and will be useful for applications further down your medical career. You can gain a placement by applying through programs such as the Nuffield Bursary scheme which organises and funds student research, or by writing directly to universities to arrange a project yourself.

Work experience: This is an essential aspect of any medical student's application. You can gain work experience at a hospital by phoning or writing to them, through your local GP, a family friend or via your school and its alumni. Alternatively you can get involved with other forms of care in the community such as nursing homes or working with children. Finding work experience can be difficult and universities are aware of this. What an interviewer will be seeking to determine is not where you did your placement but instead whether you have a realistic or a fanciful idea of what a life in medicine would be like. Consequently, rather than the quality or quantity of your work experience; it is your insight that will be key.

Societies: Joining societies and holding committee positions are excellent ways of developing your leadership, teamwork and communicative skills. Try to join charities, student mentoring schemes and science societies in your school; if it doesn't have any, all the better – start your own. This will look far more impressive than simply joining one as it shows both initiative and creativity.

Emmanuel College Gardens, Cambridge

The Application Process

Your application will be handled by the Universities & Colleges Admissions Service: UCAS. It is comprised of several parts, requiring personal information, your academic record (GCSEs and A level results), a reference and a personal statement.

The personal statement is the part you will certainly spend the most time on: 47 lines or 4,000 characters that provide medical schools with their first insight into your motivations, interests, talents and personality. Its importance does vary between universities; several use it as a tool to screen and select students for interviews, in which case a carefully written personal statement can make all the difference.

What do Oxbridge want?

There is no ideal candidate nor is there a perfect personal statement. There are however some traits that Oxbridge do look for:

- Drive and determination, both of which are essential if you are to excel in Oxbridge and become a Doctor.
- A robust student who can multitask, cope with pressure, and hopefully will 'survive' all 6 years of the course.
- An interest in academia, science based medicine and research.
- A unique feature, experience or talent that makes the student stand out.
- A structured, concise and clearly written personal statement. This is particularly important as most examinations in Oxbridge are essay based; colleges therefore look for students who write well.

Structuring your statement:

The structure and content of your personal statement will depend on your motivations, healthcare experiences, interests and of course, writing style. Here is a possible structure that you could use:

Paragraph 1 - Why you want to do Medicine:

Your first line is an important one as it will definitely be read. Keep it punchy and summarise your key motivations for becoming a Doctor. It is important to be honest, but not gushy: stay clear of cliché's such as "I want to help people" and overly sentimental sentences. Your motivations may be based on a personal experience, an interest in medical sciences, or simply because you believe your skillset is suited to the vocation, in any case keep the first paragraph clear and concise. Be aware of the fact that if you say you are primarily motivated by wanting to help people, an interviewer may reasonably ask why you want to become a Doctor rather than a nurse.

Paragraph 2 - Experiences of the Healthcare system:

This is where you can provide evidence for your particular interests in the medical field. You should try to discuss your voluntary or work experience placements rather than simply list them. Mention where they were, how long they lasted, and most importantly what you learnt from them and how they contributed to your motivations to become a Doctor.

Paragraph 3 - Academia, Medical Science and Research:

This is particularly important for an Oxbridge application and with the right content, can be very impressive. Try to mention journals or books you have read, research or lab work you have performed, and any prizes or academic achievements you have been awarded. Finally, indicate how these have strengthened your interest in the medical sciences.

Paragraph 4 - Interests and Relevant Skills:
Here you can include any clubs, societies, sports, musical instruments etc. that have developed you as a person. Several Medical Schools will be looking to see how you link these activities to three primary skills that are relevant to medicine:

- Leadership and positions of responsibility e.g. captaincy of a sport team, presidency of a committee, community work, Prefect responsibilities etc.
- Teamwork e.g. sport teams, committees, musical ensembles, organising school events etc.
- Communication e.g. presentations, debating, drama, societies etc.

Importantly, these activities not only show that you are multi-dimensional but that you can balance a successful academic profile with several other pursuits; a clear advantage over someone with only academic achievements.

Paragraph 5 - Conclusion: This should be a brief summary of your motivations and why you are suited to the profession – keep it short and snappy!

Final tips
Have a look at other personal statements from relatives, students in the years above, or online examples (useful websites can be found in the 'Resources and Websites' section of this guide); ask yourself "what are the strengths and weaknesses of this personal statement? How could it be improved?" and apply these principles to your own statement.

- Get feedback from Science teachers, friends, family and importantly an English teacher who will be able to identify grammatical or stylistic errors.
- If possible ask a tutor at an Oxbridge open day what for them constitutes a good personal statement.
- Be honest. If for example you have mitigating circumstances which have affected your academic performance make sure they have been declared in your application, either in your own personal statement or in your school's reference.
- Start early. Draft and re-draft your personal statement well before the deadline so that there's plenty of time to amend and improve.

Student profile: What tips would you give on personal statement writing?

Everyone's personal statement is different. I ordered my statement as follows: I began with a short clear sentence about what I wanted to study at university and why. This was followed by a larger section on experience and accomplishments that related to my subject. I would follow each experience/achievements with what qualities and skills I gained from them - e.g. teamwork, organisation. I then followed this with more general experience and positions of responsibility that illustrated that I was a well-rounded and reliable individual (i.e. not directly related to my subject). Finally I briefly mentioned my interests, for example musical instruments I play, clubs/organisations I was part of and sports/leisure activities. I also took a gap year so I briefly included my reasons for it, what I planned to do over the year and what I hoped to gain from it. Finally, I ended with a short, snappy summarising sentence.

Importantly, before your interview make sure you look over your statement and read up on anything that you may have mentioned in your statement. For example if you mentioned reading a scientific journal or seeing a particular medical condition on your work experience make sure you can discuss the topic as your interviewers may choose to ask you about it.

Dharshika, St. John's College, Oxford

Green Templeton College, Oxford

14.

BioMedical Admissions Test

What is it?
Following UCAS applications you will need to sit for the Biomedical Admissions Test (BMAT) in early November. It is a two-hour paper comprising of three separate sections: Scientific Aptitude; Scientific Knowledge; and Writing Skills. The test plays an extremely important role in determining whether students are shortlisted for interview at Oxbridge and ultimately offered a place. Consequently it is key that you perform well in the BMAT – just be sure to start your preparation early.

How can I prepare?
Many teachers suggest that there is little preparation you can do for the BMAT. This however is misleading; a key resource is the 'Official Guide to the BioMedical Admissions Test' by John Butterworth & Dr Geoff Thwaites, beyond that you will quickly find that each section appeals to specific skills which you can certainly develop with practice.

Section I: Scientific Aptitude
60 minutes
This section contains a number of short answer or multiple choice questions (MCQs) and aims to test your problem solving capacity and data analysis. Typically there are three types of questions:

1. Small or large texts after which there will be a single or set of MCQs to answer. They will test your understanding of any proposed arguments, their flaws, assumptions and conclusions.
2. Graphs or statistics.
3. Mathematical problems.

To prepare for these questions you should therefore focus on:

- Being able to read through texts quickly whilst absorbing key points. This can be practised quite easily with articles from journals or even newspapers. You could also ask a friend to read an article and set you questions to be completed under timed conditions.
- Improving your mental arithmetic skills. Considering that time is limited and that unlike GCSEs and A levels no calculators are allowed you must make sure that your mathematical skills are as sharp as possible – you do not want to run out of time simply because you cannot calculate the answers quickly enough. This can be practised by setting yourself a series of maths sums.

Practice questions for the Scientific Aptitude section can be found on the BMAT and Cambridge Thinking Skills Assessment (TSA) websites. Try to do them under timed conditions.

Finally, as with any test, exam technique plays an important role; here are a few tips:

- When answering MCQs you can either a) know the answer before reading the possibilities as is the case for some mathematical questions b) look for the correct answer c) eliminate unlikely answers. Use the latter two in conjunction with one another to answer questions you are unsure about.
- Section I comprises of around 35 questions, giving you approximately 1 minute 40 seconds per question. Do not spend longer than this; if you dwell on a question you will not have time to look at questions at the end of the paper which you may find easier to answer. Alternatively you can quickly move through the paper and answer all of the 'easier' questions which should take you around 1 minute each, after which you can go back and spend more time (~2 minutes) on the ones you've left out.
- If you don't know the answer – guess! There is no negative marking so don't leave anything out.
- Take a watch.

Section II: Scientific Knowledge
30 minutes
This section is commonly underestimated by students; although questions are based on GCSE level knowledge they can be tricky. There are 27 questions in short answer or MCQ format, meaning that there is considerably more time pressure than in Section I. Fast mental arithmetic, reading and factual recall is a must. When preparing make sure to review your GCSE science notes and if possible use the biology, chemistry and physics GCSE textbooks recommended on the official BMAT website. Again, there is no negative marking so answer all the questions.

Section III: Writing Skills
30 minutes

This section requires you to answer one of three essay questions on only one side of paper. It is important because:

1. It can be given priority in some colleges as it has immediate relevance to the essay-based examination system.
2. It requires you to answer questions on just one side of paper – this is a definite change for students studying essay based subjects and levels the playing field for those who do not. As a result there is significant scope to improve your performance by practising.

Sample essays are provided on the BMAT website and in the 'Official guide to the Biomedical Admissions Test'. These will show you how you should be writing and the type of content you may want to incorporate. You can then write practice essays by obtaining titles from past or specimen papers, and from the list below which primarily consists of controversial quotations, followed by a directive on how to respond: this often takes the form of 'What do you understand by this proposition? Present an argument to the contrary. How might you reconcile these views?':

- No good deed goes unpunished.
- It is irrational to regard the mind as distinct from the body.
- If the facts don't fit the theory, change the facts.
- In questions of science, the authority of a thousand is not worth the humble reasoning of a single individual.
- Censorship reflects a society's lack of confidence in itself.
- We don't live in a world of reality; we live in a world of perceptions.
- Chance favours the prepared mind.
- Progress must always be welcomed.
- Are Doctors scientists?
- Modern living is bad for our health.

In practising, a good approach is to first try to clarify your argument by answering the question in just three short sentences; it is then relatively easy to expand this into a longer, but still coherent, response.

Try to show any essays you've done to a teacher (specialising in English or the Sciences). Once you have completed the majority of the above-mentioned essay titles you should have sufficient content to apply to at least one of the questions you encounter in the BMAT. Examiners will be looking for well constructed, coherent answers that are written using good English and that explicitly answer the question set by making valid points.

Final tips

- Start preparing early – it's an important test.
- There is significant time pressure – get used to answering questions quickly.
- Practice as much as you can – it is possible to significantly improve your score.

Student profile: Do you think preparation for the BMAT is important? How did you prepare?

I think getting used to the format of the questions is important for the BMAT. In other words getting into the habit of eliminating wrong answers quickly in a MCQ is a useful skill to learn. There are a lot of questions to cover in a short space of time and recognising which questions you can't do is important too. Both these skills I think require doing practice questions rather than getting formal teaching on topics.

I didn't have much experience of doing this at A level so I did practice MCQs from a BMAT guide and I attended a course on the BMAT that my school sponsored – both of these were very helpful.

Saurabh, Downing College, Cambridge

Interviews

The interview is a key part of your Oxbridge application, that when combined with your GCSE, AS level and BMAT results in addition to your personal statement and reference, will determine whether you are offered a place. It allows the interviewers to see what type of person you are, how much you understand and crucially, how you think, in addition to helping them assess your ability independently of how well you happen to have been taught. Furthermore, it is your opportunity to sell yourself and prove that you really do deserve a place at Oxbridge. Applicants however do tend to over-estimate its importance: it is not something to get over-anxious about, as it is only one of many factors that a college will be considering.

At Cambridge, you will have two or three interviews at a given college, each with different tutors who will ask you a series of academic questions and probe your answers. Sometimes you may also have a general interview where you can be asked about your personal statement, motivations and how you will contribute to college life. At Oxford, you will be interviewed by two colleges, your college of preference and a college chosen algorithmically by the university. Neither college will be aware of your preference until after the selection process is completed. This is done to ensure fairness in the admissions process.

In several cases students being interviewed at a given college will be asked similar questions so that tutors can accurately compare applicants. Although what they are looking for will vary from person to person, tutors will undoubtedly be asking themselves the following questions:

Are you suitable? As with all interviews Oxbridge and beyond, interviewers are looking for someone who is personable, well organised and attentive. Try to relax, and importantly, build mutual trust and rapport.

Are you academically able? This is obviously a key factor in the interview. Tutors are looking for students who are not only bright but can think aloud in a clear and logical manner, presenting their opinions and defending them in a structured argument. Most important, when presented with new material, or a particularly challenging question, do your eyes light up?

Will you interact well in small group teaching? Your interviewers will contribute to at least a year of your college teaching should you be accepted, they therefore will be trying to assess your 'teachability'; how receptive you are to questions and how well you engage in academic discussions. Consequently try to be comfortable with expressing your thoughts and opinions in the interview, do not restrict yourself simply because you don't want to be criticised – give the tutors an opportunity to know you and realise that you are a motivated person who they will want to teach.

Are you interested in medicine and well informed? These are obvious qualities that you will need to display in all of your interviews at each university you apply to. Interviewers want to see you are passionate about a career in medicine, and that you've been doing the necessary reading to reflect that. They may ask you about any books or journals you read, breakthroughs that have been shown in the news and any research or work experience you may have done – be very prepared!

Can you communicate? As a doctor you will need to communicate with a range of people: patients from a variety of backgrounds, nurses, fellow doctors, senior consultants and researchers. Tutors are therefore looking for students who can articulate their thoughts and feelings clearly and concisely, being able to discuss and explain complex concepts in a logical and comprehensible manner.

How can I prepare?

The topics that will be covered in your interviews can be broadly categorised into a) medical sciences b) ethics, policy and law c) you and your personal statement. These questions need different approaches:

Medical Sciences

Across Oxbridge, questions on the medical sciences are the most common but also the widest ranging. Typically questions tend to extrapolate from your A level biology or chemistry courses, or lead to topics covered in the first year of medicine. It is therefore important that you understand and are comfortable with the concepts covered in your entire A level syllabus, even parts your school may not have covered yet, and can apply your knowledge to unfamiliar situations. You should also familiarise yourself with basic medical science – several websites cover such material, these can be found in the 'Resources and Websites' section of this guide.

Knowing the answer however is only half the battle, you must be able to think aloud, answering questions clearly and logically – remember, interviewers care much more about how you arrive at an answer rather than the answer you arrive at. When you are asked a question, try to use the following algorithm:

1. Take your time and think
2. Simplify and break down the question into its key parts, mention these to the interviewer
3. Sequentially and logically answer each part
4. Summarise your argument or opinion

As you answer the question interviewers will frequently try to prompt or guide you – listen carefully to their hints and use them to shape your argument. Most important of all, do not be put off by what the interviewer says or treat their comments as criticisms – always be constructive.

Question: How do enzymes in the pancreas digest food in the gut without digesting the pancreas itself? What would happen to the body if these mechanisms failed?

BREAK DOWN	1. Enzymes are active in the gut but not the pancreas – how is this possible?	2. What happens when the pancreas is damaged or autodigested?
LOGIC	The difference lies in the location. Enzymes in the pancreas are not exposed to the fluid found in the gut. ↓ Perhaps something in the gut fluid activates the enzymes. ↓ What's found in the gut fluid? Other enzymes, pH buffers etc. ↓ Enzymes in the gut could activate pancreatic enzymes by cleaving them into an active form. Alternatively the enzymes could become activated by the different pH in the gut.	There will be a response to the damage e.g. pain and inflammation. Additionally the functions of the pancreas will be impaired. ↓ The pancreas is both an exocrine organ producing pancreatic juice and an endocrine organ producing hormones (e.g. insulin) – both could be impaired. ↓ Reduced release of pancreatic juice into the gut could alter the digestion of food. The contents of the juice e.g. amylases could even be forced to enter the blood. ↓ Impaired release of hormones such as insulin alter blood glucose levels.

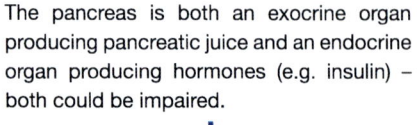

SUMMARY: Enzymes released by the pancreas are not active as they have not been activated by the gut fluid. If they were to become active in the pancreas, a patient could suffer from pain, altered blood glucose and pancreatic enzymes could be present in their blood.

Finally, practise answering such questions as much as you can either in front of a friend or to a teacher. You can find Oxbridge questions online or in any databases your school might have. The best source however is older students who have already had Oxbridge interviews and can tell you about their own personal experiences. These insights are typically very useful, but keep in mind that questions can change from year to year.

Here are a few example questions to get you started:

Chemistry:
- How do K^+ ion channels achieve selectivity of K^+ over Na^+ and Mg^{2+} ions?
- Why are humans made of carbon?
- Why do the colours of halogens change down the periodic table?
- What is special about water?

Biology:
- Do foetal lungs receive blood? Through which vessels?
- Why is blood pressure important?
- What is negative and positive feedback? Give examples in the body.
- What common problems seen by a GP are due to the fact that we are bipedal rather than quadripedal?
- How do we localise sounds?
- How many DNA bases encode an amino acid? (3) Why not 2 or 4?
- Why is diabetes bad?
- How are electrical signals generated and conducted in neurons?
- How can we apply Ohm's law to the cardiovascular system?

Physics:
- How would you explain to a child what an atom was?
- Why is the sky blue?
- Why are electrical conductors usually opaque?

Remember, science questions can be much more interactive – many interviewers show students graphs, microscope images or even objects such as a skull asking them to describe the object and determine its origin or function.

Ethics, Policy and Law

Beyond the medical sciences, interviewers frequently test your ability to tackle ethical situations that Doctors commonly face, and more large-scale political problems found in the NHS. Most of the time a clear head, rational thinking and common sense will suffice to produce a competent argument. To impress the examiner however you may want to deepen your knowledge of these topics and keep abreast of recent changes by reading articles found in the Student BMJ and broadsheet newspapers. It would also be useful to look through the General Medical Council's online guidance on 'Good Medical Practice' (refer to the 'Resources and Websites' section of this guide) and to read books such as 'Medical Ethics: A Very Short Introduction' by Tony Hope. Aim to follow a similar framework to that mentioned above when answering ethical questions, be logical, state the key ethical issues presented in the question, address them systematically, discuss both sides of the argument and summarise your answer. Most importantly, steer your answer towards a discussion, build a rapport with the interviewer and try to connect.

You and your personal statement

Interviewers will spend most of their time trying to assess how you think. Frequently however, candidates are asked more general questions about themselves and their personal statement in order to determine their motivations and how well they will fit into college life – in some cases an entire interview is dedicated to this. Consequently it is important that you are prepared to talk about why you want to be a Doctor and are thoroughly familiar with your personal statement, being able to explain for example why you did an activity, what you learnt from it and which of your skills it improved. Here are a few questions which you might be expected to answer:

- What are the disadvantages of a medical career?
- Talk to me about a patient you saw during your work experience?
- Why did you take... (your non-science A level subject)?
- Tell me about an article you read recently?
- Which scientist over the past century do you most admire?
- How do you keep motivated?
- Is there more to medicine than applied science?
- How do you cope with stress?
- How do you manage your time?

Given the scientific nature of the Oxbridge courses, an interviewer will want to know whether you really understand how they differ from other medical courses, and whether you have a genuine enthusiasm for this approach.

Final Tips

Before Interview-Day
- Practise answering questions aloud as much as you can – ask teachers, friends or family to question you and provide feedback on your responses.

On the Day
- Sleep & eat well, stay hydrated, arrive early.
- Dress in smart casual clothes that you are comfortable in. Try not to wear anything you might fiddle with under interview stress.

In the Interview
- When you meet your interviewer, open with a firm handshake; sit with your palms open on your legs, your back straight, knees bent and feet well grounded. Try not to cross your arms or legs – the aim is to use positive body language.
- Smile and relax. Keep eye contact and project your voice.
- Don't rush to respond, take your time, think about your answer and then speak.
- Think clearly and out aloud, if the interviewer criticises, disagrees or tries to put you off don't worry - they simply want to see how you cope under pressure.
- Try to be different and show original thinking in your answers, interviewers are looking for students who can provide novel insights into basic concepts.
- Stand out and be memorable, establish a 'connection' with the interviewer. In most cases if the interviewer likes you, you will get a place.
- Be enthusiastic about tackling challenging questions – enjoy the process. This is arguably the single most important factor: it may help to know that many candidates have said how extraordinarily stimulating and interesting the interview was – they really did enjoy it!

After the Interview
- Do not discuss what you have been asked with other interviewees.
- If an interview doesn't go well, don't worry, focus on the next one.

Student profile: What tips would you give for interview preparation?

The biggest advice I'd give anyone is to be yourself! You're not expected to answer all the questions or even understand all the concepts thrown at you. Treat the interview as a discussion, which hopefully you should find interesting. In terms of your preparation, make sure you go through your personal statement with a fine tooth comb, because they could potentially pick on anything you've mentioned. The medical interviews are extremely scientific, but try not to spend all your time reading through your A level notes as questions can often go beyond the syllabus.

Arif, New College, Oxford

Student profile: What were you asked in your Oxbridge interviews?

My first Cambridge interview was with the college admissions tutor who was a really nice guy; the interview was just a friendly chat about my interests (and the classic question: "what do you think you can contribute to..." - in this case, Selwyn College) rather than an aptitude test. The second interview was with a tutor and Professor at the College. I was asked many scientific questions covering the cardiovascular system, flow through blood vessels, protein carriers in cell membranes and glucose transport into cells. For each question I was also given a diagram or graph to explain. The questions didn't require anything more than A level knowledge, but many of the questions did require some thinking and working through. The final interview involved a lot of debate over ethical issues. I was asked for my views on animal testing and blood transfusions for Jehovah's witnesses.

Christina, Selwyn College, Cambridge

Student profile: What were you asked in your interview and what advice would you give to prospective students on interview preparation?

I had two interviews for Medicine at Emmanuel College. The first was similar to interviews at other universities. There was a GP and a Fellow and the questions began on the topic of my work experience in General Practice. From there, they went on to ask about more points from my personal statement, such as an essay competition I had won on the future role of Doctors and how I thought these roles would develop in the coming years. At this point, the GP handed over to the Fellow who started asking scientific questions about neurological disorders (linked to the neurology work experience I had carried out). The questions were tough but were built up slowly enough to be accessible even to A level students.

The second interview was entirely dissimilar to the typical medical interview at other universities. It was completely science oriented and consisted of each of the interviewers leading me through a 'scientific puzzle'. The first was to do with esters and general chemistry while the second was to do with proteins.

It's important to remember that they're really interested in how you thnk. I got many questions wrong in my interview but I made sure that I was constantly explaining my thought processes. As long as they see that these processes are logical and clear, it's not important whether you end up reaching the right answer or not. Make sure you know your own personal statement inside out but don't do too much background scientific reading other than brushing up on your A level material. You won't be able to predict the scientific questions they ask. Also, remember to relax. There are a lot of bizarre rumours about Oxbridge interviews and this has a tendency to unnerve a lot of prospective students. Try to think of the interview as more of a 'trial tutorial/supervision', a conversation in which you're trying to express your own scientific ideas, rather than an interrogation!

Finally, don't think about the interview after coming out. Out of 18 medics in my college, probably 15 were convinced (myself included) that we wouldn't get in based on our interviews!

Myura, Emmanuel College, Cambridge

All Souls College, Oxford

Resources & Websites

Universities
Cambridge
University website for prospective students: www.cam.ac.uk/admissions/undergraduate/courses/medicine/
Student Union website for prospective students: www.cusu.cam.ac.uk/prospective/
Oxford
University website for prospective students: www.ox.ac.uk/admissions/undergraduate_courses/courses/medicine/medicine.html
Student Union website for prospective students: www.ousu.org/prospective-students

Colleges
Cambridge
Official prospectus: www.cam.ac.uk/admissions/undergraduate/colleges/index.html
Alternative prospectus: www.cusu.cam.ac.uk/prospective/prospectus/
Oxford
Official prospectus: www.ox.ac.uk/admissions/undergraduate_courses/colleges/
Alternative prospectus: www.ousu.org/prospective-students/ap/

Personal statement writing
Advice: www.medschoolsonline.co.uk/index.php?pageid=108
Examples: www.studential.com/personalstatements/getpscourse.asp?type=36
Examples: www.personalstatement.info/
Examples: www.thestudentroom.co.uk/wiki/Category:Medicine_Personal_Statements

BMAT
Official website: www.admissionstests.cambridgeassessment.org.uk/adt/
Thinking Skills Assessment website: www.admissionstests.cambridgeassessment.org.uk/adt/tsacambridge
USA Scholastic Aptitude Test website: sat.collegeboard.com/practice

Interviews
General
Profiles: www.oxbridge-admissions.info/
Ethics
Good medical practice: www.gmc-uk.org/guidance/good_medical_practice/index.asp
Student BMJ archive: student.bmj.com/topics/non-clinical/medical_ethics.php
Science
Google eBook: Physiology by Linda S. Costanzo
Wikipedia
Student BMJ (non clinical section): student.bmj.com/topics/topics.php#global

Teaching Courses
www.oxbridgeapplications.com/
www.kaptest.co.uk/

Useful forums
www.thestudentroom.co.uk/
www.admissionsforum.net/
www.newmediamedicine.com
www.studentdiscussion.co.uk/

Useful journals
student.bmj.com/
www.nature.com/
www.sciam.com/
www.newscientist.com/

Sponsors and Supporting Organisations

'Oxbridge Medicine: The Applicant's Guide' has been generously supported and assisted by several medical societies and organisations:

Cambridge University Medical Society
The Cambridge University Medical Society (CUMedSoc) represents all students of the university's Medical School. It was established to liaise with the university and the town's people on behalf of the student body but has since grown. Aside from having a strong say in the way course is organised and run, CUMedsoc plays an important role in other aspects of student life, from arranging discounts for books at local retailers to running workshops to help new students. In addition the society provides subject related travel grants to support students, as well as organising a number of social events throughout the year for members.

Cambridge University MedSIN
MedSIN Cambridge is a student organisation that raises awareness and action for humanitarian and global health issues locally and internationally. It provides talks, summer placement information and campaigning opportunities to its members.

Oxford Society for Medicine
Oxford Society for Medicine is a student society dedicated to promoting debate on the key issues in modern medicine. The Society hosts high profile speaker events on issues ranging from cutting edge science to current medical careers and politics.

The Osler House Club
The Osler House Club is the primary organisation supporting all clinical medical students at Oxford University. They provide welfare, academic and social support for the clinical medics in addition to Osler House itself, a building with meeting, dining, games and club rooms.

Medical Protection Society
The MPS is the world's largest medical defence organisation, providing the best possible protection and peace of mind for medical professionals throughout their careers. With more than 265,000 members and a team of highly-skilled staff, MPS is the leading provider of comprehensive professional indemnity and expert advice to doctors, dentists and health professionals in the UK and around the world.